SUPERUSELESS SUPERPOWERS.

ADOLFO ALCALA, PATRICK CONLON, JASON NITTI, & NEEL WILLIAMS.

WITH ILLUSTRATIONS BY MARK TODD

"IF WITH GREAT POWER COMES GREAT RESPONSIBILITY, THESE PEOPLE HAVE A LOT OF FREE TIME."

sourcebooks

Published by Sourcebooks, Inc.
P.O. Box 4410, Naperville, Illinois 60567-4410
(630) 961-3900
Fax: (630) 961-2168
www.sourcebooks.com

Library of Congress Cataloging-in-Publication Data

Superuseless superpowers / Adolfo Alcala … [et al.] ; with illustrations by Mark Todd.
  p. cm.
Collected from the blog, Superuseless.blogspot.com.
1. Heroes—Humor. 2. Supernatural—Humor. I. Alcala, Adolfo. II. Superuseless.blogspot.com.
PN6231.H44S87 2011
791.45'652—dc22

2010047806

Printed and bound in the United States of America.
VP 10 9 8 7 6 5 4 3 2 1

Dedicated to our proofrearder, Derek

INTRODUCTION

Greetings good reader! Or as they say in Europe, "hi." This book chronicles many people, but it really begins with one man. Charles Darwin. Unless you live under a rock or in certain parts of the Florida panhandle, you know that Charles Darwin came up with a newfangled theory called natural selection, aka, survival of the fittest.

But what if Darwin was wrong.

(Pause for dramatic gasp and outcries of "Oh no you di'int!")

What if evolution could take a giant side step? Well, actually a step that's sideways and a little backwards. The kind of step you'd take if you were in a long line and the person in front of you farted, so you step back and are all like, "Oh jeez that's disgusting," but you don't want to step so far away that you lose your place in line. So yeah—a step like that.

Anyway, we started noticing something strange about two years ago. People with oddly evolved abilities. Abilities that were so mundane, so uninspiring, so ironic...that they could only be described as Superuseless.

And so our mission began. Armed with only our bad instincts and a thirst for the truth, we traveled the world to uncover these quasi-superheroes. The following pages contain nearly everything we collected along our way, including a lot of made-up stuff.

So, friends...suspend your disbelief...and dive headfirst into the extremely shallow waters that are...

SUPERUSELESS

SUPERPOWERS

13TH BULLET
BULLETPROOF.

Bang, Bang, Bang, Bang, Bang, Bang, Bang, Bang, Bang, Bang, Bang, Bang, Boink.

THE TWINVISIBLES.

HALF INVISIBILITY   99% OPACITY

Double the useless, double the stupidity. Born in the fallout of the Chernobyl disaster, the Twinvisibles came to America as part of a high school exchange program. One twin has the power to turn 99% opaque (or 1% invisible). The other is half-invisible. That is, he's only invisible to the left eye. But when these unamazing forces combine... well, you get a couple of dudes who could only sneak up on Helen Keller. (What? Too soon?)

GRIM LEAPER

GRIM LEAPER.

Able to leap tall buildings in a single bound? That's just weak. The Grim Leaper can jump over anything on earth. Problem is, once he jumps he never comes back down. Watch as he soars over houses! Over skyscrapers! Over clouds and planes! Then burns up in the Earth's atmosphere. (Sigh.)

The ancients say the original Grim Leaper's first (and last) jump happened on a moonless evening.
A constellation, "Jumpus Onceicus," marks the spot where he was last seen silhouetted against the night sky.

Atmosphere 3000

MAKE GRAVITY YOUR BITCH.

OFFICIAL FOOTWEAR OF THE GRIM LEAPER*

*50,000 ft. vertical leap not typical.

Mutations in Our Modern Genetic Makeup and Their Causes

BY PHILLIP GREENBAUM
SPECIAL CORRESPONDENT

Over the past decade, we at the Society of Scientists Studying Stuff have carefully observed a genetic phenomenon resulting in what some have called "Superuseless Superpowers." With the aid of a microscope and several lab assistants from Sweden, we have examined a number of test subjects who exhibit traits of this curious condition.

The first studies revealed nothing genetically unique about our test subjects. Indeed, our prospects looked quite dark. But then we discovered that someone accidentally left the lens cap on the microscope. After this breakthrough, we soon found what came to be known as the "Superuseless Gene."

To explain the sudden appearance of this gene across the globe, we began by conducting a series of trials on lab rats. Gamma rays, carbon monoxide, large slabs of bacon… nothing seemed to trigger the SU Gene. Until one day one of our assistants was watching television in the lab. A reality TV show, to be exact. That afternoon our lab subjects began exhibiting distinct signs of superuseless behavior. The next day we introduced several more televisions into the lab environment, each tuned to a different reality show. The amplified variable led to similar increases in superuseless activity, therefore establishing a clear link in causality.

> *Gamma rays, carbon monoxide, large slabs of bacon…nothing seemed to trigger the SU Gene.*

It is our finding, then, that the sudden appearance of Superuseless Superpowers is due entirely to the increasing popularity of reality television shows. The inherent stupidity of said programming has inundated our bodies with what can only be described as quantum stupidity, small bursts of intense idiocy that cause normally healthy genes to become lazy, indolent, and also rather fat. Over time, these new mutated genes become what we have identified as Superuseless.

Oh, and I'm not a real scientist.

SUB-ZERO

SUB-ZERO.

Stick a submarine sandwich in the toaster and "whoa doggie!" you've got yourself a taste sensation. Which makes the Sub-Zero power all the more disappointing, because its corresponding hero automatically untoasts any toasted sub. Alas, the warm, gooey goodness of melted cheese and crisp crunch of toasted baguette are mere fantasies to Sub-Zero. So sad. So...untoasty.

HEALING PUNCH

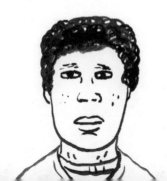

HEALING PUNCH.

Float like a butterfly and sting like the bedside manner of Mother Teresa. Whereas most strong punches deliver a crushing Ivan Drago-like knockout, your ferocious fists instantly heal the damage you inflict, leaving your opponent feeling refreshed and rejuvenated.

BRUTAL FISTFIGHT INJURES NONE!

By Ron Rockwell

RICHMOND — At 1:14 a.m. this morning a donnybrook took place outside of local watering hole, Commerical Tap House. Witnesses claim that it all began when one of the inebriated combatants began lobbing insults at the other. "He was all like, 'Your Momma's so fat, she broke her leg and gravy came pouring out,'" said Edward Baldwin, a Tap House regular. He further explained, "I haven't heard that razz since 1994, so needless to say I was pretty shocked."

At this point, the victim of the aforementioned razz suggested that they take the quarrel elsewhere. Both men staggered outside.

The razzer exited first, followed by the razz-ee. Before a small crowd could even form around the men, the razzer turned around and threw what appeared to be a haymaker/sucker-punch that connected directly with his victim's jaw.

But instead of falling to the ground like a sack of potatoes, the punch victim appeared to be rejuvenated. "I couldn't believe it," said one bystander. "One second he's getting beat down, and the next, he looks like he just had 9 hours of rest on a Sleep Number mattress. Those things look real comfortable, ya know?" Confused and tired, the crowd disbanded, as did the two men. No further incidents occurred.

PANTSFORMER

PANTSFORMER.

Most superheroes put their pants on one leg at a time, just like you and me. Unless, of course, they are the pants. Meet Pantsformer! In the zip of a fly, he can transform into any pair of pants. Flat-front, pleated, boot cut, Hammer...you name it. Just don't ask him to turn into capri pants. It's a personal thing.

1. Hemmed.

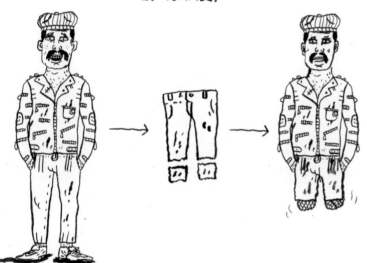

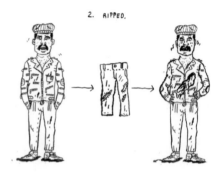

2. RIPPED.

3. ACID WASH.

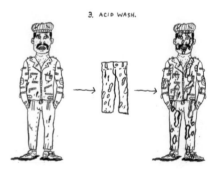

USELESS

TALES

{PANTSFORMER}

Glen lay there between the silk bed sheets, fondling his moustache and eyeing the naked woman next to him. He still felt a little winded after performing his signature sexual maneuver. Something he liked to call "The Lazy Toucan."

He grabbed a picture frame off the bedside table and examined it. Inside the frame was a candid snapshot of Russel J. Vandekamp. The sight of Mr. Vandekamp's absurdly obvious comb-over and fat, sweaty face caused Glen to snicker.

"I wish you wouldn't touch that picture," Mrs. Vandekamp said. "What if he saw your fingerprints or something?"

"Ha! He's an accountant, honey, not Magnum P. I."

Mrs. Vandekamp sat up, then slipped on her terry cloth slippers monogrammed with a crimson letter "V."

"I'm gonna go take a shower," she said, sashaying towards the bathroom. Glen admired the gentle wobble of her behind, perfectly shaped over thousands of hours in the pilates studio. Seriously, what was her husband thinking, leaving her alone so much of the time? Glen half wanted to punch the guy and half wanted to shake his hand for being such a...

The door downstairs creaked open and shut. In an instant, 10,000 volts of electricity ran up and down Glen's spine. He then heard the unmistakable shuffle of Mr. Vandekamp's black orthopedic sneakers across the foyer floor.

Glen checked his watch. 3:37 p.m. What the hell was this guy doing here? Oh Christ. Now he heard footsteps coming up the stairs. Without wasting another second, Glen quickly transformed into a pair of navy blue sweatpants. Maybe being the Pantsformer wasn't so useless after all. Especially in a jam like this.

Mr. Vandekamp flung open the door and announced, "Rita, it's me."

A sharp scream of surprise echoed from the shower. "What?! Russ?"

"Just thought I'd surprise ya. Make sure you weren't cheatin' on me."

"Ha, don't be silly," she responded with a look of sheer terror that he could not see.

Mrs. Vandekamp quickly threw on her bathrobe and appeared in the bedroom.

"What are these?" Mr. Vandekamp asked, pointing at the pair of sweat pants on the bed.

She immediately knew that the pants were, in fact, her lover. She thought back to the first time she had met Glen—in a department store changing room. Pervert that he was, Glen had hung on a rack waiting for some young hottie to slip him on. His ruse had worked well. Very well, indeed.

Unable to concoct a story, she fumbled her words: "Uhhhh, they're...they're...for you!"

He studied the pants for a moment, then held them up to his sweaty lower torso. Seeming satisfied, he sat on the edge of the bed and began taking off his shoes.

"Thank Christ," Glen thought, "the fat bastard's gonna take a nap." But as soon as Russel Vandekamp undressed down to his skivvies, he proceeded to slip on the sweat pants. Glen now found himself face to face with Vandekamp's testicles, and what could only be described as the smell of rancid bacon-flavored mayonnaise.

"Whoa, Russ baby...what are you doing?" his wife asked, trying to hide her true panic.

"Ya know what? I'm gonna do a few miles on the old exercise bike. Haven't used that thing in years!"

Several hours later, Glen, in human form once again, is curled in the fetal position beneath a cold shower.

Some things, as they say, can never be washed off.

INFINI-MASON

INFINI-Mason.

Like the song says, "All we are is just another brick in the wall." And by we, we mean Infini-Mason, who has the power to morph into a mighty brick wall! But much like watching a Michael Bay movie, it's only good once, thus our hero stays a brick wall forever. On a related note, did you know that the Berlin Wall was actually named Heinrich? True story.

Obituaries, cont. from pg. 1A

survived by her husband and newborn baby.

Hollis Blumenthal, 46

Johnson City, TN - The JCMC medical examiner confirmed earlier today that Hollister Hubert Blumenthal passed away at 8:30 a.m. Blumenthal caused controversy in 1998 due to his failed superheroics. In a futile attempt to protect

Hollis H. Blumenthal

the city from a tornado, Blumenthal turned himself into a brick wall. Forever. The tornado, predictably, passed over Blumenthal leaving millions of dollars in destruction. Moreover, the Blumenthal wall prohibited relief workers from quick access to tornado victims.

Blumenthal had been living in the same spot for the past 11 years, until city commissioners voted unanimously to tear down Blumenthal to allow for a proposed Steak & Ale.

He is survived by his brother Gerald Blumenthal. There will be a service on Monday when his ashes and debris will be scattered in the old quarry.

Ant. 25-176

IN MEMORIAM

INFINI·MASON

(1976-1997)

"HERE ONCE STOOD A WALL THAT WAS A MAN
THAT IS NOW MARKED BY THIS, ANOTHER WALL"

MEMORIAL WALL

EMO-RTAL

EMO-RTAL.

We all grow out of our phases, right? Well, not everyone. Meet Anne Arky, an emo-chick with an eternal lifespan forever stuck at the age of 15. Hundreds of years from now she'll still be sporting T-shirts of heartbroken nasal singers who whine about their rich dads' summer homes in Rhode Island. Immortality hasn't come in handy for her, aside from the small perk of being a cutter who doesn't bleed.

Sham-meh.

POWERPOINTER.

Nothing says "I have nothing to say" like the popular medium known as PowerPoint. And this superuseless ability lets you blow hot air in style. The Powerpointer is able to take any situation, from a trip to the bathroom to getting a cavity filled, and immediately turn it into a slideshow-friendly presentation. Too bad he works at a coffee shop, 'cause he could climb the corporate ladder stupid fast.

WEREWOOF,

TOUGH.

We all have a beast within. Some beasts just don't grow out of their adorable puppy stage. Whenever the full disk of the moon is illuminated, this man-beast transforms into his cuddly, pint-sized, non-threatening alter-ego. He doesn't snarl, nor does he foam at the mouth. But if you whistle ever so softly, he'll roll over and let you scratch his were-belly. Oh, and when he howls at the moon, it's just the most darling thing.

THE TREADMILLION DOLLAR MAN

You'd think that being the Treadmillion Dollar Man—having superhuman speed only when running in place—would have its rewards. But you'd be wrong. Most heroes with this power have been found working as Phys Ed instructors or waist-down fitness models. Which gives new meaning to the old phrase "getting nowhere fast." (NOTE: This power is not to be confused with "Stationery Speed," which is the ability to write thank-you notes at a mind-boggling pace.)

As evidenced by his prized dance trophy, Treadmillion Dollar Man totally owned the 80's.

ULTRA SHORT RANGE TELEPORTATION

ULTRA SHORT RANGE
TELEPORTATION.

Being able to get away from any situation is quite useful. Getting an inch away from that situation, now that's useless. Thus the curse of Ultra Short Range Teleportation, the power to teleport up to an inch (or 2.54 cm if you're one of those pompous metric lovers). The good news is that, when done in rapid succession, it can really push your "popping & locking" routine to the next level.

FLAMERANG

FLAMERANG.

While on holiday in the Outback, baby Angus was snatched from his mum's arms by dingoes, then left for dead. Luckily, he was rescued by aborigines who raised him as one of their own. Growing up, he discovered that he could harness the power of the guwiyang—the aboriginal word for fire. One problem: the guwiyang balls he shoots always return to their point of origin. Angus is currently preparing for Aussie grunge band Silverchair's comeback concert. He'll be providing pyrotechnics. It's a one-time gig.

This gem is the useless third cousin to the classic useful power called Laser Vision. Those afflicted with Laser Pointer Vision have a gaze that isn't strong enough to burn through objects, only strong enough to point them out. Prolonged eye contact is still highly dangerous, not to mention a little awkward.

USELESS

TALES

{LASER POINTER VISION}

The time was 7:56 a.m. The car was a Ford Cirrus. Mike Tyre pulled into his parking space outside the sad two-story building known as "WP Corporate Headquarters." Though he'd worked there for five years, Mike still had no idea what "W" and "P" actually stood for. He was middle management. Expendable. Mediocre in all aspects. If Wednesday were a person, Mike would be it.

All this was about to change.

The WP weekly status meeting always started at 8:30 a.m. Sharp. With just minutes to go, Mike set up his laptop projector in Conference Room 4 while the meeting attendees slugged back office coffee like it was oxygen. Spirits were high and artificial dairy creamer was running low.

The lights dimmed. The room silenced. Mike brought up slide one: the words "Good Morning" next to a clipart illustration of a coffee cup. This was a tactic Mark learned at an airport Marriott seminar called "Professional Presenters Present: The Presenting Presentations Presentation." Or was it at the Holiday Inn? Either way, one of the first lessons of the seminar (also conducted in PowerPoint) was to form an early bond with your audience. And thanks to Mike's judicious use of clipart, his audience was now putty in his very soft, slightly undersized hands.

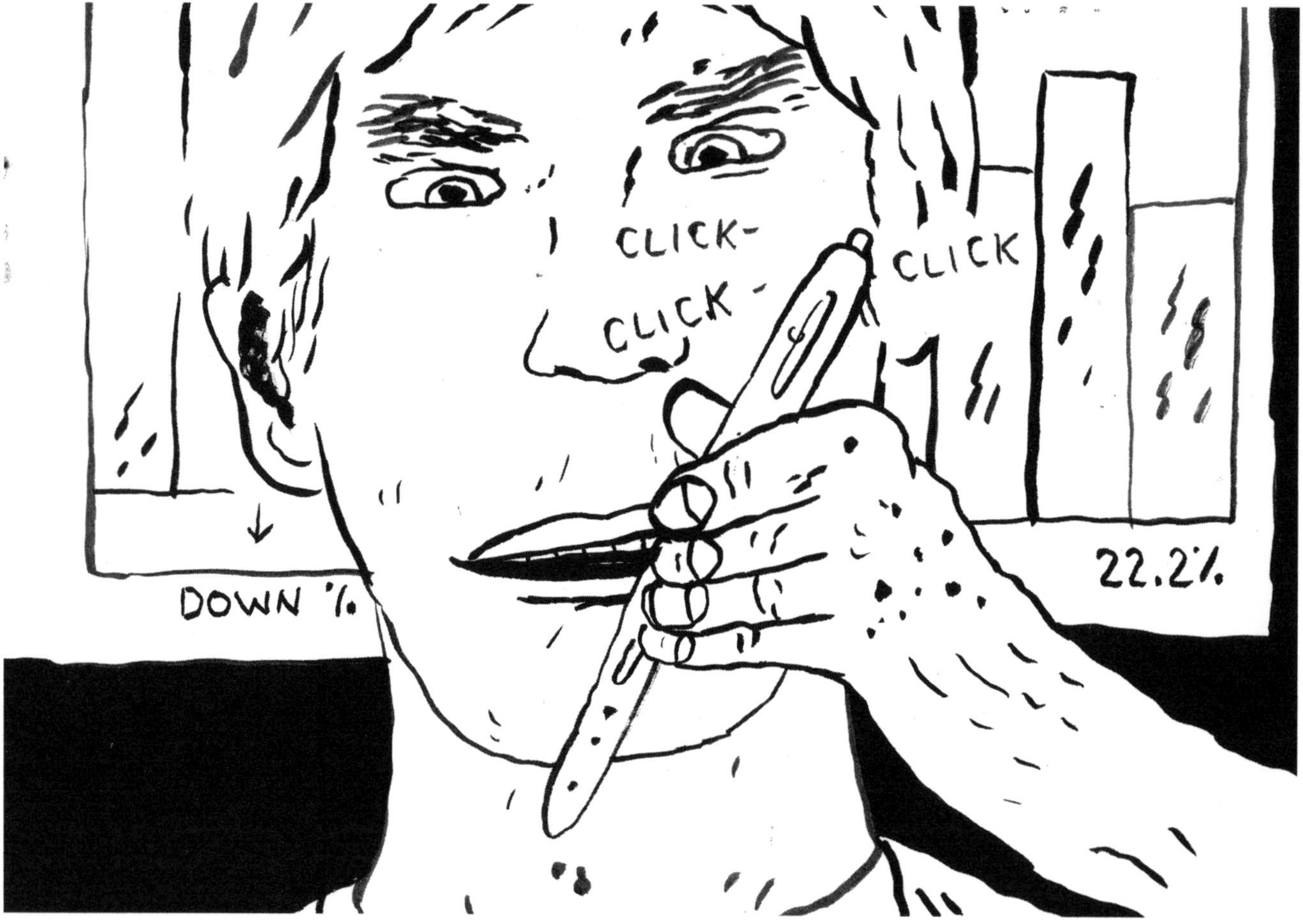
CLICK-
CLICK-
CLICK
DOWN %
22.2%

Moving on to slide two. A simple bar graph. Mike now unsheathed his secret weapon—the Penpoint 3000, purchased out of a Skymawl catalogue while on a trip to Akron, Ohio. For only $37.45, plus $12.99 shipping and handling, Mike procured not a pen, not a laser pointer, but a pen-slash-laser-pointer. Who cared that it weighed just under half a pound and gave him Carpal Tunnel after only a week of use? There were also the irregularly shaped moles that began appearing on his writing hand, but nevermind all that.

Now with the Penpoint 3000 in hand, Mike engaged the red laser and gestured towards the center of his graph. But where the PP3K had succeeded so many times before, its precise red beam now failed. Mike laughed nervously. He shook the pen and tried again. Nothing. He could hear several of his coworkers shift their weight in the ergonomic office chairs. He shook the pen even harder now. Still nothing. Now on the verge of desperation, Mike did what any man would do. He held the laser up to his eye and viciously clicked the on/off button.

And so it happened. The event that would alter his life. Forever.

Mike's rapid clicking caused the pen's laser to fire. The red, concentrated beam entered his pupil at its exact dead center. Dazed, he stumbled around with his hand over his eye. His vision began to clear after a few seconds. But something felt different. Something was...wrong. Everywhere he looked he saw two small, red dots. A collective gasp erupted throughout the conference room.

"What?" Mike asked. "What's wrong?"

And thus—in the not-blink of an eye—Laser Pointer Vision was born!

TELEKINNEARSIS

TELEKINNEARSIS.

Sue Miller may look like your average lonely woman who wears heart-shaped pendants and writes in a diary. But she also has the world's only known case of Telekinnearsis—the power to move actor Greg Kinnear with her mind! Unfortunately, Kinnear is the only thing she can move. So, you know...bummer.

Actor breaks leg, for real

HOLLYWOOD — Early last evening, actor Greg Kinnear was rushed to the hospital after an incident on a Hollywood backlot. Witnesses say he left the hospital on crutches several hours later. His left leg appeared to be in a cast. This is the latest in a bizarre series of events involving the actor, dating all the way to 1995 when Kinnear sailed into the air at the Cable Ace Awards.

Actor Kinnear

Certain right-wing religious sects have even gone so far as to boycott Kinnear's films. Jebediah Mills, leader of The Original Orthodox Baptist Churches of Northwestern Mississippi, went on record saying, "Greg is an instrument of the dark lord. I'm not just talking about the floating in the air thing. I mean, he was in that terrible movie "Baby Mama." So that ought to tell you something."

An unnamed crew member on yesterday's set claims to have seen a very similar situation to what was caught on film in 1995. "One second he's delivering his lines on-camera and the next he's floating up in the studio rafters. I've seen some weird sh*t, especially when I shot that music video with Michael Bolton, but this is like the weirdest."

As of press time, Kinnear's camp could not be reached for comments.

Premomnition.

This power takes "mama's boy" to a whole new, extremely disturbing, and often times perverse level. Those cursed with Premomnition are able to see what their mother is doing. At all times. From what we understand, it works kind of like picture-in-picture on big screen television sets. Sure, you may love your mom now, but wait until you try having sex while your mom's baking cookies. Or maybe you're into that kind of stuff. Sicko.

Distracted by the apparition of his mother on laundry day, our hero gets pwned.

M O M BIEN®
(OEDIPALARIUM TRANQUILATE)

Too much mommy time? Not enough you time?

Finally there's a better way! It's called Mombien...from the makers of Dadquil. Simply grind up a Mombien tablet and slip the powder into your mother's favorite drink. Within minutes she'll be in a deep, restful sleep lasting 4-12 hours. If sleep lasts longer than 5 days, please consult a physician as a coma might have occurred. Imagine, no more seeing your mom take a shower while you're trying to give a work presentation. It's time to live your life the way you want to—with your mom sleeping peacefully at the edge of your field of vision. Ask your doctor about Mombien to receive a free trial pack TODAY!

Mombien.
When mom's out cold, you can be bold!

TO THE GIRL WHO PUTS THE "HER" IN HERBIVORE

I spotted you at the organic farmer's market in Park Slope, Brooklyn. Your hair was the fiery orange color of gluten-free sweet potato puree. Your eyes the emerald hue of dill pickle popcorn seasoning. As I turned to place the assorted pack of gourmet non-allergen chutney in my eco-friendly reusable bag made of recycled Crocs material, you disappeared. If you are out there, let's meet again.
☎ ▓▓▓▓▓▓▓▓▓▓▓

DID YOU KNOW MOM UPSIDE-DOWN SPELLS WOW? NOW YOU DO.

It was Ladies Night at Mulligan's. The night was awash with early-2000s U2. Y'know, the epic "uno-dos-tres-catorce" stuff. As I slammed down my third Jager-kicker of the night, I saw you out of my peripheral. You looked just like my mother. Well, actually you were standing in just the right place where your body matched up with my mom's face. [Sidenote: My mother is always in my field of vision.] But, man-oh-man, you had the most amazing body. More curves than the 4-leaf clover the bartender carved into the foam of my milk stout beer. If you by chance see this, please meet me at Mulligan's next Thursday. ☎ ▓▓▓▓▓▓▓▓▓

ELEPHANT HIDE-US

ELEPHANT HIDE-US.

This power enables its superhero to bend the very fabric of space and time through teleportation! The kicker is that you can teleport to one place, and one place only...an elephant's colon. An elephant named "Pancake" at the San Diego Zoo, to be exact. We recommend an hour-long shower and several months of therapy after each teleportation experience.

When He Goes Missing, Stop the Kissing.

BY INGRID BLIXT

DEAR INGRID: My boyfriend is really sweet and affectionate. But sometimes he'll just disappear. I'll start talking about my biological clock and then, poof, he literally vanishes. I won't see him for days and then he comes home smelling like raw sewage. What should I do?

Rebecca – Chicago, IL

DEAR REBECCA: Same old story, Becca. Your bf fears commitment like every other man on earth. Cut him loose! As for the vanishing act, my only explanation is that he's a magician moonlighting as a septic tank technician. Either go out there and get yourself a real man or go sit on the washing machine.

*

DEAR INGRID: My office coffee tastes terrible. Should I complain to someone, or just suck it up and keep buying $4 lattes from the coffee store next door?

Jillian – Bismarck, ND

DEAR JILLIAN: When I used to drive an 18-wheeler on the ice roads of Alaska, I'd get all hopped up on amphetamines then drive until I couldn't stand the smell of my own body fluids. So, to answer your question, Jillian, I'd just bring your own French press to work and brew it at your desk. People will think you're an arrogant prick and you'll probably get promoted into middle management.

*

DEAR INGRID: Our neighbor's dog barks all night long. As a result, my 6 year-old can barely sleep at night which means she's falling asleep at school. I've mentioned it several times to the neighbor but he hasn't seemed to do anything. Any advice?

Sally – Tacoma, WA

DEAR SALLY: So here's what you do. You get yourself some rat poison and a shovel. Next, you go over to the...okay, just kidding. Seriously, you must have thought I was going to tell you to poison the dog. Ha! So what you really do is frame the neighbor as the kingpin of an illegal child-bride smuggling ring. He and his dog will most likely be beaten by the police and put away for life. Then it's no more dog, plus the prospect of a new, more attentive neighbor. You're welcome!

*

TELE-APATHY

Tele-Apathy.

Who hasn't wanted to read minds at one point or another? But be careful what you wish for, as Tele-apathetics can only read people's boring thoughts. No sexy musings. No international secrets. Just "Did I leave the iron on?" broadcasting 500 times a day. Yikes.

THAT GUY

THAT GUY.

picture
not
available.

You've probably seen him before. In the mall. On the bus. Perhaps on a repeat of any show playing on the USA network during the last decade. He's That Guy. The power of That Guy allows its hero to be so utterly unremarkable and average in every way that no one can recall anything about him. Most superheroes ask themselves, "Who am I?" in an existential way. That Guy asks himself the same question, but in a "No, really. Who are you?" kind of way.

PUDDLE GILLS

PUDDLE GILLS.

This superhero is a direct descendant of Poseidon. But 3,000 years of titan/god inbreeding have diluted his mighty genes to produce just one ability—breathing underwater, but only water up to a ½ inch deep. Puddle Gills currently lives as a Greek Mythologian Fundamentalist sect leader in Athens, Georgia along with his fully-armored amphibian sidekick, Warfrog. Together, they wait for rain. But not too much rain.

JUANITA APPENDIX

JUANITA APPENDICITIS.
A.K.A. JUANITA APPENDIX.

Vestigial is one of those words you just
don't get to see enough. Vestigial. Vestigial. Vestigial.
There, that's better. And this power concerns the
most well-known vestigial organ of all—the appendix.
You see, Juanita Appendicitis has an appendix that
naturally regenerates. Trouble is, her super organ is
awfully temperamental and prone to inflammation.
Hooray for general anesthesia.

NON-JITSU

NON-JITSU.

Never be seen. It's the first rule of the ninja, right above: "Always store your katana sword with silica packets to prevent moisture damage." And while this hero has the powers of superhuman stealth and mastery of martial arts, he also suffers from a nasty case of nyctophobia—fear of the dark. So whenever he's out launching his sneak attacks under the cover of night, his enemies always get a nice 240-watt warning announcing his tiptoeing presence.

NO-GO-LIATH

NO-GO-LIATH.

Bigger, stronger, but definitely not faster. When this hero "powers up," his body grows to gargantuan size while his feet remain exactly the same. Upon reaching full height, No-Go-Liath inevitably topples to the ground like freshmen at a fraternity kegger. Until they come up with a tank-sized motorized wheelchair, this dude is a gigantic doorstop.

FLAWGIC

FLAWGIC.

Imagine being able to construct a logical argument so tight, it'd make Aristotle wet his toga. Now imagine the only time you can do this is when talking to an angry girlfriend. (Cue sad trombone.) Now you know the plight of the Flawgic power. As we all know, logic has no measurable effect on significant others. Especially when talk turns to feelings. Which it always does. Dammit.

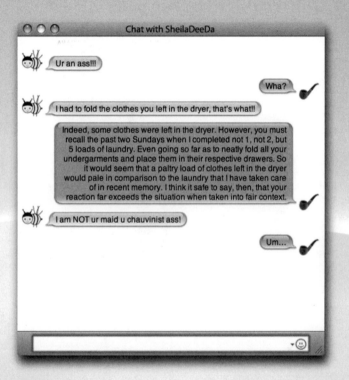

Chat with SheilaDeeDa

Ur an ass!!!

Wha?

I had to fold the clothes you left in the dryer, that's what!!

Indeed, some clothes were left in the dryer. However, you must recall the past two Sundays when I completed not 1, not 2, but 5 loads of laundry. Even going so far as to neatly fold all your undergarments and place them in their respective drawers. So it would seem that a paltry load of clothes left in the dryer would pale in comparison to the laundry that I have taken care of in recent memory. I think it safe to say, then, that your reaction far exceeds the situation when taken into fair context.

I am NOT ur maid u chauvinist ass!

Um...

Brain

IM transcripts

IN-FLIGHT FLIGHT.

Being able to soar through the air still won't save you from recycled oxygen and strangers' life stories. Known as the "Cabin Sparrow," this power lets you fly, but only within the confines of an airplane. Being able to leapfrog the beverage cart when explosive diarrhea strikes at 30,000 feet is sort of a plus, though.

CUSHNECK ®

The world's first
aerodynamic neck pillow.
Using traditional neck
pillow technology, we added
the word "aerodynamic"
and doubled the price. Now
feel your comfort reach new
heights. Get it? Heights.
You get it, right?

$48.33

PSYCHIC AMNESIA

PSYCHIC AMNESIA.

Crystal balls. Peep stones. Tarot cards. These are the tools of the trade of many a clairvoyant. But this seer of the future should try carrying around a memo pad. Every time he has a psychic vision, he immediately suffers an episode of anterograde amnesia. Too bad, because he's ESP'd on everything from natural disasters to coup d'etaws to French typos to the obligatory 2019 Oscar nom for Lou Diamond Phillips. Sometimes he predicts visions of himself predicting visions of himself having a prediction which he instantly forgets. Wait, what?

SLUMBERJACK

SLUMBERJACK.

Sleep is a time to relax, recharge, and have a recurring sexual fantasy involving cream-filled donuts. That is, unless you have the power of the Slumberjack, whose strength turns superhuman as soon as he hits REM sleep. The trail of sleepwalking destruction can be annoying, but it makes for an excellent excuse to forgo post-coital snuggling.

STREET MEETS

Researchers have hit the pavement to survey the public's reaction to the emergence of Superuseless Superheroes. Here's the word on the street.

ANONYMOUS
PROFFESIONAL BLOG
COMMENTER

"I bet when you have Eventual
Kevlar Skin your elbows can get
pretty ashy."

DIANE & EARL
OLD PEOPLE

"Slumberjack? We're still rooting for
him to one day find his Slumberjill."

DAISY BROWN
SOCIALITE

"I've seen Pantsformer. He's ultra
cute. Tell him I'm size 8 in Jordache!"

WALK THROUGH WALLISH

WALK THROUGH WALLISH.

You vibrate your atoms. Pass your atoms between other atoms. Molecular mumbo-jumbo ensues. In layman's terms, you can walk through walls. Well, guess what? That layman is a dick. Because your walk-through-walls power only lets you go about yay-far before you thunk into the opposite side of the wall you just entered. Welcome to sheetrock purgatory.

SHADOWFLEX

SHADOWFLEX.

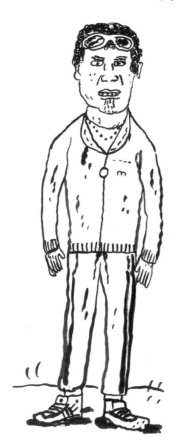

When it comes to shadowplay, rabbits and reindeer are yesterday's news. The unamazing power of Shadowflex allows its hero to cast the shadow of a Home Gym. Unfortunately, the shadow alone does nothing for creating oily, hairless, and well-defined pectorals. To get those, Shadowflex has to pay four easy installments of $49.99 just like the rest of us.

SUPERUSELESS

SUPERPOWERS.COM

About the Authors.

Adolfo, Patrick, Jason, and Neel became friends while working in the creative department at the same Madison Avenue advertising agency [insert joke about "being useless for a living" here]. The quartet was impregnated with the superuseless concept while on a lunch break one day. Nine months, and several dozen inebriated conversations later, superuseless came screaming into the world via the blog superuseless.blogspot.com. The blog became a viral success, and hey, now it's a book. Damn, I can't believe you're still reading this.

PATRICK.   ADOLFO.   JASON.   NEEL.

About the Artist.

Mark Todd is the proud owner of two first names. In 1993 he graduated with honors from Art Center College of Design in Pasadena, California. Upon realizing that Pasadena isn't actually in Los Angeles, he moved to New York, where he worked for clients like MTV, Coca-Cola, SONY, the *New Yorker*, and The MTA. In 2003 he moved back to Southern California with his wife and fellow artist, Esther Pearl Watson, along with their daughter Lili.

When he's not wasting his talents by doing illustrations for a book like this, Mark stays busy with gallery exhibitions, teaching at ACCD, and creating work for clients like *McSweeney's* and the *New York Times*. He is the author of the popular children's book, *Monster Trucks!*, as well as *Whatcha Mean, What's a Zine?*, a book about creating zines and mini-comics.

MARK.